A Crabtree Branches Book

Today's Stars

ZENDAYA

Ellen Rodger

Crabtree Publishing

crabtreebooks.com

School-to-Home Support for Caregivers and Teachers

This high-interest book is designed to motivate striving students with engaging topics while building fluency, vocabulary, and an interest in reading. Here are a few questions and activities to help the reader build upon his or her comprehension skills.

Before Reading:

- *What do I think this book is about?*
- *What do I know about this topic?*
- *What do I want to learn about this topic?*
- *Why am I reading this book?*

During Reading:

- *I wonder why...*
- *I'm curious to know...*
- *How is this like something I already know?*
- *What have I learned so far?*

After Reading:

- *What was the author trying to teach me?*
- *What are some details?*
- *How did the photographs and captions help me understand more?*
- *Read the book again and look for the vocabulary words.*
- *What questions do I still have?*

Extension Activities:

- *What was your favorite part of the book? Write a paragraph on it.*
- *Draw a picture of your favorite thing you learned from the book.*

TABLE OF CONTENTS

YOUNG AND TALENTED

Actress, singer, dancer, model—Zendaya was all of these things before she even turned 20! She is also an **activist** who supports many causes and charities.

In 2020, at the age of 24, Zendaya won the Primetime **Emmy Award** for Outstanding Lead Actress for her role in *Euphoria*. She was the youngest woman to win the award! She won it again two years later.

Away from the spotlight, Zendaya is quiet and private about her life. But as a well-known entertainer, she also feels it is important to speak out to help others who could benefit from her power and **influence**.

Fun Facts

Zendaya became a **vegetarian** not because she loves vegetables, but because she loves animals.

EARLY DAYS

Zendaya Maree Stoermer Coleman was born on September 1, 1996, to Claire Stoermer and Kazembe Ajamu Coleman. She grew up in Oakland, California, within a big family that includes three stepsisters and two stepbrothers.

Zendaya's father quit his job as a teacher to become her manager.

Fun Facts

Zendaya's name combines "zen," for peace, with the southern African Shona-language word *tendayi*, for "give thanks."

In her video "Z for Zendaya," Zendaya talks about her roots as a biracial American with German and African ancestry.

As a child, Zendaya loved to sing, act, and dance. At six, she and her friends acted in a play for Black History Month. At eight, Zendaya joined a hip-hop dance group called Future Shock Oakland.

To further pursue her interest in performing, Zendaya joined theater groups. She also attended a school for the arts. These early experiences gave her the skills and confidence to continue a career in performing arts.

For many young artists who want to follow a path in performing arts, theater groups can be the starting point of their journey.

FRESH FACE

Zendaya began modeling for department store ads at 13. Soon after, she launched her professional acting career, appearing on Disney Channel shows. Her first was the show *Shake It Up*.

Zendaya played a young dancer named Rocky Blue in Shake It Up.

While acting and attending school, Zendaya appeared in music videos and released her own music. At 15, her single "Watch Me" reached 86 on the Billboard Hot 100.

Zendaya's first album, Zendaya, *was released in 2013. It consisted of 12 songs, many of them featuring themes of love and heartbreak.*

Soon, Zendaya was appearing in movies, on television, and on Hollywood red carpets. Her sense of style had people taking notice too.

*One of Zendaya's first major fashion moments was at the 87th **Academy Awards**, or Oscars, in 2015.*

Fun Facts

Toy company Mattel produced a Zendaya Barbie doll dressed in Zendaya's designer clothing as she appeared at the 2015 Oscars.

Zendaya's hard work and talent brought her bigger movie and TV roles. In 2017, she appeared in the movie *Spider-Man: Homecoming*. **Critics** called her a scene stealer.

Zendaya met fellow actor Tom Holland (right) on the Spider-Man: Homecoming *set. He played the role of Spider-Man and she played Michelle (MJ), his love interest. They later became a real-life couple.*

Zendaya continued her role as MJ in *Spider-Man: Far from Home* (2019) and *Spider-Man: No Way Home* (2021). She also began winning awards for her acting, and making waves for her public appearances.

Spider-Man: Far from Home *was one of the highest-earning movies of 2019.*

In 2019, Zendaya began starring on the television show *Euphoria*. She earned praise for her role on the series. It also brought her acting awards, including two Primetime Emmys and a **Golden Globe Award**.

Zendaya also became one of *Euphoria's* executive **producers**. This means she has a greater role in making decisions about the show. She has written and performed music for *Euphoria* and was nominated for two Emmy Awards for Outstanding Original Music and Lyrics.

In Euphoria, *Zendaya plays a teenager named Rue who struggles with drug addiction and feeling out of place.*

BRANCHING OUT

Creating and producing television shows and movies at a young age is unusual. But Zendaya is known for her many talents and keen ambition. In 2021, she helped create, produced, and starred in the film *Malcolm & Marie*.

Zendaya donated some of the proceeds from Malcolm & Marie *to the food bank organization Feeding America.*

One of Zendaya's most well-known roles was in the two *Dune* movies. They showed her broad range of acting skills.

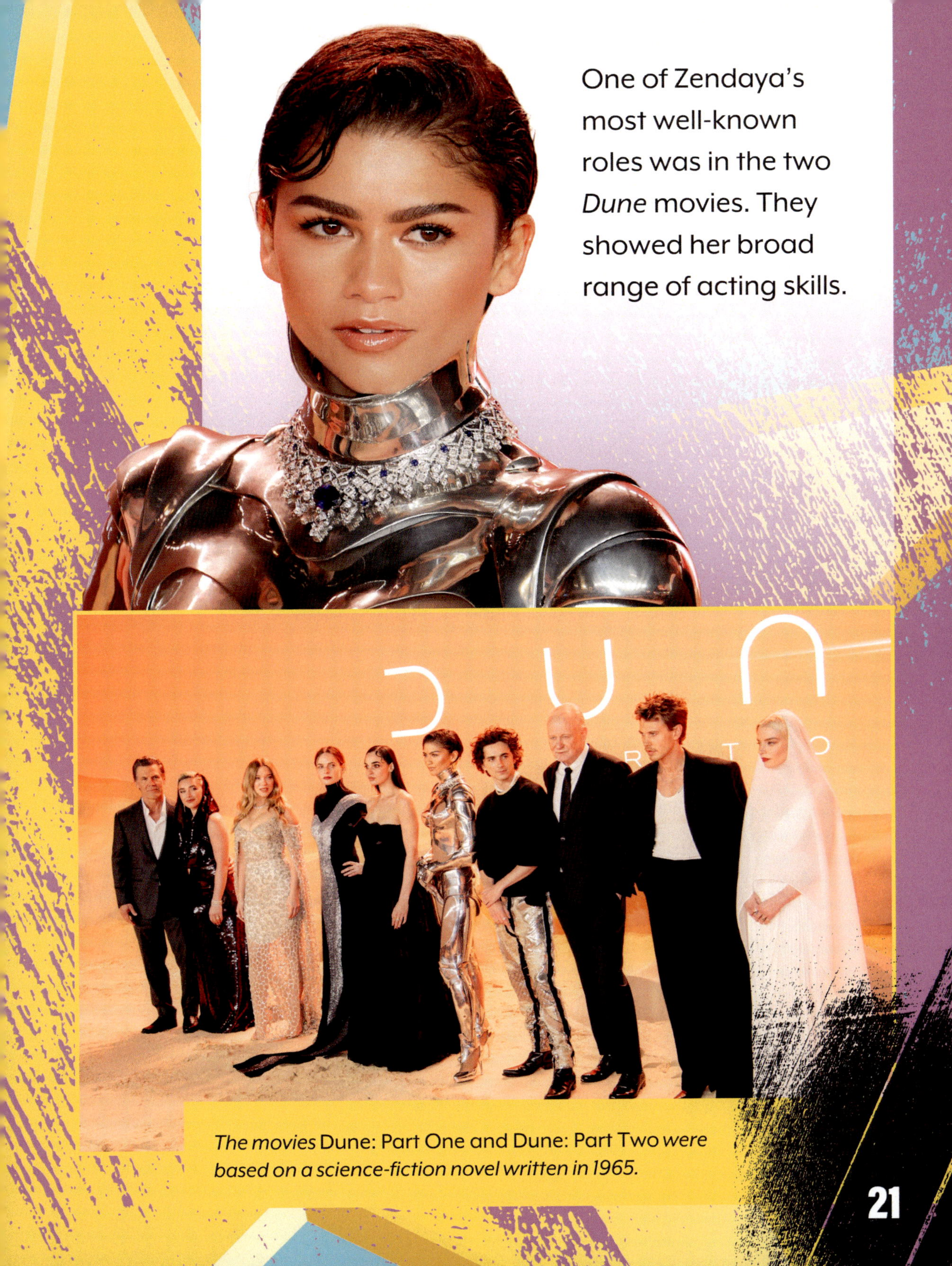

The movies Dune: Part One *and* Dune: Part Two *were based on a science-fiction novel written in 1965.*

Zendaya has appeared in dramas, comedies, documentaries, and music videos, and has voiced animated films. Her likeness has appeared in the video game Fortnite Battle Royale. Zendaya is also a music artist and dancer. She headlined her own concert tour from 2012 to 2014.

Zendaya has made guest appearances in music videos by artists such as Taylor Swift.

Fun Facts

As a kid, Zendaya was a big fan of the animated movie *Space Jam*. As an adult, she used her voice-acting talent in the role of Lola Bunny in *Space Jam: A New Legacy*.

LIFTING AS SHE RISES

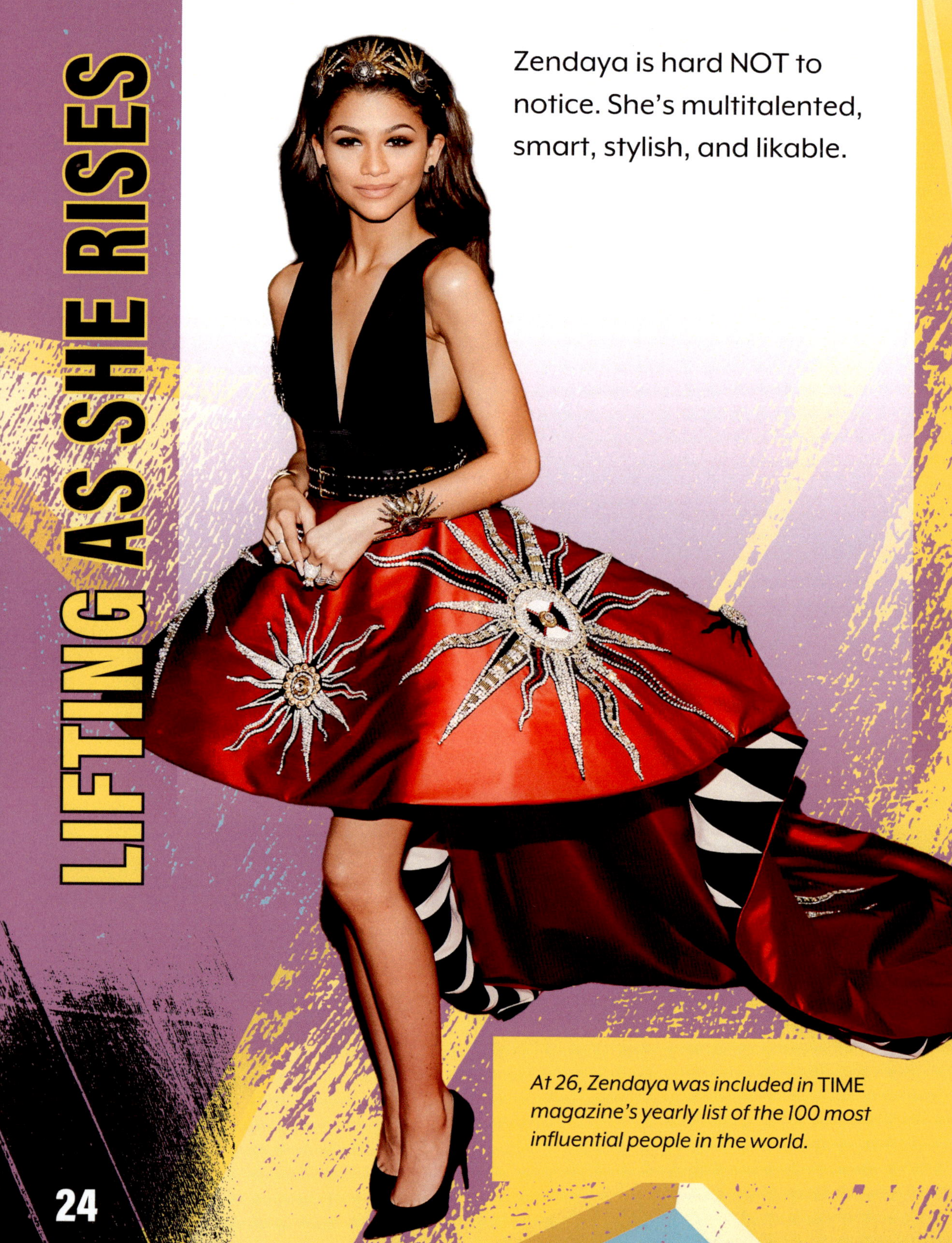

Zendaya is hard NOT to notice. She's multitalented, smart, stylish, and likable.

At 26, Zendaya was included in TIME *magazine's yearly list of the 100 most influential people in the world.*

The entertainment magazine *Variety* included her on its list of the 500 most influential entertainers in the world. When she appears on the red carpet, she always makes news for what she wears and what she does.

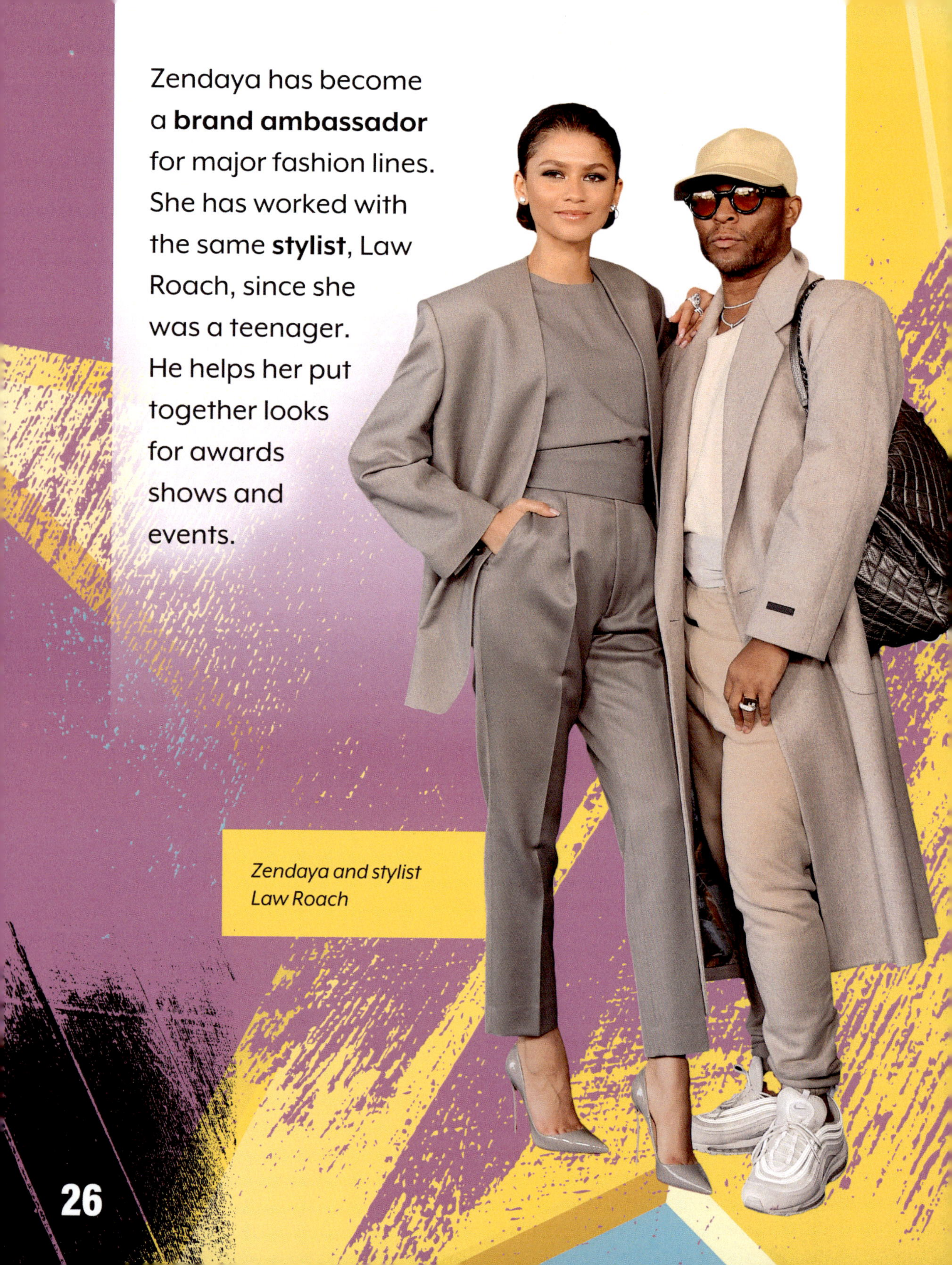

Zendaya has become a **brand ambassador** for major fashion lines. She has worked with the same **stylist**, Law Roach, since she was a teenager. He helps her put together looks for awards shows and events.

Zendaya and stylist Law Roach

Fun Facts

The Council of Fashion Designers of America made Zendaya the youngest person ever to win its Fashion Icon award in 2020.

Zendaya has used her fame to promote and support many causes and charities. She is vocal about fighting for **racial equality** and women's rights.

Zendaya celebrates International Day of the Girl Child in New York City on October 11, 2018. This is an annual celebration to champion the rights of girls worldwide.

One way Zendaya chooses to help others is by promoting the work of Black women and creators. Another is by giving time and money to charities that support children with AIDS. Zendaya also raises awareness against bullying and has helped with disaster relief groups.

Zendaya has given her support to many causes, and she encourages others to do the same.

GLOSSARY

Academy Awards (uh-KAD-uh-mee uh-WAWRDS): An annual awards ceremony for the movie industry

activist (AK-tuh-vist): Someone who uses action to push for a cause

brand ambassador (brand am-BAS-uh-dawr): A person who is chosen to represent or promote a certain brand or product

critic (KRIT-ik): A person who gives opinions about movies, books, or other forms of art

Emmy Award (EM-ee uh-WAWRD): An award for outstanding achievement in television in the United States

Golden Globe Award (GOHL-duhn glohb uh-WAWRD): An award for outstanding achievement in international film or television

influence (IN-floo-uhns): The power to have an important effect on someone or something

producer (pruh-DOO-ser): A person who oversees the making of a movie or television show

racial equality (REY-shuhl ih-KWOL-i-tee): When people of all races are treated in an equal manner

stylist (STAHY-list): A person who understands fashion and helps others develop style and looks

vegetarian (vej-i-TAIR-ee-uhn): A person who does not eat meat, or in some cases, food from animals, such as eggs, milk, or cheese

INDEX

WEBSITES TO VISIT

https://www.zendaya.com

https://kids.britannica.com/students/article/Zendaya/634758

https://kids.kiddle.co/Zendaya

ABOUT THE AUTHOR

Ellen Rodger won a bank-sponsored short story contest at age nine. It was the last thing her bank ever gave her for free, but it kicked-started a career in newspaper, magazine, and book publishing. Ellen has written hundreds of books for curious young people, on topics as varied as the history of the potato, urban wildlife, refugees, the Great Lakes, and explorers.

Crabtree Publishing

crabtreebooks.com 800-387-7650

Written by: Ellen Rodger
Designed by: Kathy Walsh
Series Development: James Earley
Editor: Melissa Boyce
Educational Consultant: Marie Lemke M.Ed.
Production manager: Candice Campbell

Hardcover: 978-1-0398-8035-1
Paperback: 978-1-0398-8395-6
Ebook (pdf): 978-1-0398-8155-6
Epub: 978-1-0398-8275-1

Printed in the U.S.A./CP2025

Published in Canada
Crabtree Publishing
616 Welland Ave.
St. Catharines, Ontario
L2M 5V6

Published in the United States
Crabtree Publishing
347 Fifth Ave
Suite 1402-145
New York, NY 10016

Library and Archives Canada Cataloguing in Publication
Available at Library and Archives Canada

Library of Congress Cataloging-in-Publication Data
Available at the Library of Congress

Photographs
Alamy: BFA p 23
Newscom: WENN p 13, Splash p 14, Columbia Pictures p 17, HOME BOX OFFICE p 19, The Reasonable Bunch p 20, SplashNews p 27, Vantagenews p 28
Shutterstock: DFree, cover, title page, p 26; Featureflash Photo Agency, TOC, p 8; Tinseltown, p 5, p 16, p 22 FashionStock.com, p 6; Omri Eliyahu, p 9 (bottom) s_bukley, p 10; Kathy Hutchins, p 12, p 15, p 29, p 31; CarlaVanWagoner, p 18; Loredana Sangiuliano, p 21 (bottom); Fred Duval, p 21 (top) ; Sky Cinema, p 24, p 25
Wikimedia: Toglenn, p 4,
All other images from Shutterstock